THE SOLDIER
THROUGH HISTORY

Peter Chrisp

with illustrations by Tony Smith

Wayland

JOURNEY THROUGH HISTORY
The Farmer Through History
The Inventor Through History
The Sailor Through History
The Soldier Through History

Series editor: William Wharfe
Editor: Rose Hill
Designer: Robert Wheeler

Typeset in the UK by Dorchester
Typesetting Group Ltd
Printed in Italy by G. Canale &
C.S.p.A., Turin

First published in 1992 by
Wayland (Publishers) Limited
61 Western Road, Hove
East Sussex BN3 1JD, England

© Copyright 1992 Wayland
(Publishers) Limited

**British Library Cataloguing in
Publication Data**
Chrisp, Peter
  Soldier Through History – (Journey
  Through History Series)
  I. Title II. Smith, Tony III. Series
  355.009

ISBN 0-7502-0383-8

Text acknowledgements
The publishers have attempted to
contact all copyright holders of the
quotations in this book, and
apologize if there have been any
oversights.
The publishers gratefully
acknowledge permission from the
following to reproduce copyright
material: Allen Lane, for an extract
from *First Day on the Somme*, by
Martin Middlebrook, 1971; Edward
Arnold, for an extract from *The
Crusades: Idea and Reality 1094-
1274*, by Louise and Jonathon Riley-
Smith, 1981; Barrie and Rockliff, for
an extract from *Russia at War 1941-5*
by Alexander Werth, 1964; Charter
Books, for an extract from *The Life of
Billy Yank, The Common Soldier of
the Union* by Bell Irvin Wiley, 1962;
Chatto & Windus, for an extract from
War in the Ancient World by Y
Garlan, 1975; Harcourt Brace & Co,
for an extract from *Sherman,
Fighting Prophet* by Lloyd Lewis,
1932; the *Observer*, for an extract
from an article by Hugh McManners,
3 March 1991; Open University
Press, for an extract from *Frederick
the Great* by T Lentin, 1979; Penguin

Books, for extracts from 1) *King
Harald's Saga*, 2) *Plutarch on
Sparta*, 3) *Plutarch's Lives*, 4) *The
Travels of Marco Polo*; Rutgers
University Press, for an extract from
The Empire of the Steppes, by R
Grosset, 1970; Sphere Books, for an
extract from *Hitler as Military
Commander*, 1971; *The Sunday
Times*, for extracts from articles on
20 January 1991 and 3 February
1991; Tressell Publications, for
extracts from *Contemporary
Accounts of the First World War* by J
Simpkin, 1981; Weidenfeld &
Nicolson, for an extract from
Chronicles of the Crusades, 1989.

Picture acknowledgements
The publisher and author wish to
thank Bridgeman Art Library 16;
C.M. Dixon 6, 9, 10; Mary Evans 26,
41; Werner Forman 22; Michael
Holford 5, 8, 17; P. Newark 20, 25,
28, 30, 32, 36, 38; Novosti Press
Agency 40; Popperfoto 34, 37, 45; R.
Sheridan 18; Topham Picture Source
42, 44. All other pictures are in the
Wayland Picture Library.

Contents

The battlefield

War has been part of human life for at least 10,000 years. During this time, the methods of fighting have changed greatly, as people have invented ever more effective ways of killing one another. But whether armed with a sword or at the controls of a tank, a soldier's role is still the same: it is to kill, and in doing so to risk death on the battlefield.

People become soldiers for many reasons. Some join because they have no choice – they are conscripted, or forced to serve, by the government. Others volunteer in order to escape poverty and unemployment. In times of war, people enlist for reasons of patriotism. There have also been many wars of religion, fought because people believed that God was on their side.

In some societies, fighting was seen as a noble activity. Aztec warriors, medieval knights and Mongol horsemen were all trained from an early age to enjoy fighting, and to see war as a way of gaining glory. For these people, war enabled them to rise in society.

Soldiers have generally been young men, for they are best able to cope with the physical ordeals of soldiering – hunger, lack of sleep and long marches carrying heavy equipment. Some young men are attracted by the thought of adventure and excitement. Even so, in the nineteenth century, there were many

This seventh century Saxon whalebone carving from Northumbria shows Egil the archer, a legendary hero, defending his wife and home against armed raiders.

Fighting for glory

In many societies, fighting has been a way of winning fame and glory. The Vikings of Scandinavia celebrated their battles in poems, which were passed on from one generation to another. Through warfare, people hoped to be remembered after their death. This is how a Viking poet called Thjodolf Arnosson sang the praises of his king, Harald of Norway (1015–66):

All men know that Harald
Fought eighteen savage
battles;
Wherever the warrior went
All hope of peace was
shattered.
The grey eagle's talons
You reddened with blood, great
king;
On all your expeditions
The hungry wolves were
feasted.
(King Harald's Saga.)

examples of women posing as men in order to enlist as soldiers. Since the Second World War, most armies have included women, although not often as frontline soldiers.

History books on war often tell us more about the overall battle plan than about life as a soldier. Historians and army generals are most concerned with who wins and who loses. But the ordinary soldier is much more concerned with staying alive. Battlefields are always noisy, with the shouts of the attacking troops, the shrieks of the wounded and the roar of the guns. Often the air is thick with smoke. The soldier is usually afraid and confused, unsure of what is happening around him. Why does he stand and fight?

Part of the answer is military discipline and the fear of punishment. In many armies, soldiers have been trained to fear their own officers more than the enemy. But the soldier also knows that his own survival depends on the tiny band of comrades who fight alongside him. He is afraid of letting them down by showing cowardice. So throughout history armies have often organized men in small groups, living and fighting side by side.

The French, led by Napoleon (on the white horse) fought the British at the Battle of Waterloo, 18 June 1815 – one incident in ten hours of fierce fighting. By the evening, 40,000 soldiers and 10,000 horses lay dead and dying on the battlefield. The soldiers of both sides were hungry, tired after a long march the previous day and they were also soaked with rain.

The battlefield
Hugh McManners, a British officer who served in the Falklands War (April–June 1982), described combat: *The battlefield is a truly terrible environment. In war, all the usual rules of society are gone. You can get away with almost every excess – until your conscience catches up . . . In battle there is no time for debate – particularly of the morality of orders . . .*

(*The Observer*, 3 March, 1991.)

A Greek hoplite

In Ancient Greece, wars were fought by foot soldiers called hoplites. This name comes from *hoplon*, the large circular shield carried by each man. The hoplite wore a bronze helmet with a horsehair crest, which made him look tall and imposing, together with a breastplate and greaves (shin guards), also of bronze. His weapons were a long wooden spear tipped with iron and a short iron sword. The spear was not thrown but was used for striking enemies.

Hoplites were part-time soldiers, drawn from Greece's middle and upper classes. Each man had to provide his own armour, and poorer Greeks could not afford it.

The hoplite went into battle in a line formation called a phalanx, a living wall of warriors with their shields interlocked. This might be several rows deep. Each man relied on his neighbour's shield to defend his right side, while he defended the hoplite on his left in the same way. During peacetime, the men would exercise and train together. Loyalty and trust were important for the hoplites, who were fighting shoulder to shoulder with their friends.

This Greek carving of a battle scene shows a phalanx advancing in the top row.

The shield

It was against the law of Sparta for a hoplite to leave his shield behind on the battlefield, but not his helmet or breastplate. According to Plutarch, King Demaratus of Sparta explained: *This is because they put on the latter (helmet and breastplate) for their own benefit, but their shields for the sake of the battle-line as a whole.* (Plutarch, *Moralia*, III, 220, 2.)

horsehair crest

bronze helmet

Aegean Sea

ASIA MINOR

Delphi

Athens

Sparta

Crete

bronze-covered
wooden shield

For the hoplites, victory depended
on bravery, strength and skill in
handling the shield and thrusting
spear.

leg shield

Persian archer

Although all the Greeks spoke the same language and worshipped the same gods, they did not belong to a single nation. Instead, they lived in independent city states, and these were often at war with each other.

They fought for many reasons, though each side always claimed that its wars were defensive. The city states often quarrelled over farmland and disputed border areas. They might also go to war if they feared that a rival city was growing too powerful. Individual Greeks hoped to win fame or glory by showing bravery. Victory in war also brought practical benefits such as captured goods and slaves.

A circular temple to Pythia at Delphi, built about 370 BC.

Laws against cowardice

In Sparta, hoplites who showed cowardice in battle were known as *tresantes*, or runaways. These quotations from the Ancient Greek Xenophon (c430–c354BC) illustrate the humiliation suffered by cowards:

At Sparta everyone would be ashamed to be associated with a coward. . . . In the streets he is required to give way, as well as to give up his seat even to younger men. . . . He must not walk around with a cheerful face: otherwise he must submit to being beaten by his betters. (*The Constitution of the Lacedaemonians*, IX, 4–6.)

It was considered a disgrace for a woman to be given to any of them [cowards] in marriage, and anybody who met them was at liberty to strike them if he chose. They were obliged to go about unwashed, to wear cloaks which were patched with rags of different colours, and to shave one half of their beards and let the other half grow. (Plutarch, *Life of Agesilaus*, XXX, 3.)

Greek wars always began with religious rituals. First the gods had to be consulted to see whether they favoured the war. The Greeks believed that the gods showed their wishes at special shrines called oracles. The most famous was the oracle of the god Apollo at Delphi. Messengers from all over Greece would travel to Delphi to ask questions of the god through his priestess, who was called the Pythia. If it seemed that the gods approved of war, heralds were sent to the rival city with a formal declaration of war.

Battles usually took place on open, level ground, for no phalanx would willingly fight uphill. At a given signal, the two lines of opposing hoplites would charge towards each other. For the greatest impact, all the Greek forces were sent into battle at once, and so fighting was usually over in a few hours. When a soldier in the front line fell, his place was taken by someone from the line behind. They would fight until one side's phalanx broke and ran. With their heavy body armour (weighing 32 kg), the victors were usually too tired to chase the defeated side once the fighting had stopped.

After the battle, the victors would strip the dead and bury the corpses on the battlefield. Then they would set up a trophy – armour hung from a tree or a carving showing the armour with an inscription celebrating victory. They would also send captured weapons and armour to their temples, offered in

Hoplites in battle with a charioteer, from a Greek vase painting.

thanks to the gods.

The most successful of all the city states in war was Sparta. The Spartans, unlike the rest of the Greeks, were well-trained, full-time soldiers. Their work was done by slaves.

Spartan boys grew up in military schools where discipline was harsh. Until the age of sixty, all Spartan men had to serve in the army. They lived in communal barracks, even when they were married.

Hoplites against cavalry

Sometimes the Greeks had to fight against foreigners, such as the Persians, who fought on horseback. But the stirrup had not yet been invented and so riders were not securely mounted. The Greek general Xenophon told his hoplites before one battle:

We are on a much more solid footing than cavalrymen, who are up in the air on horseback, and afraid not only of us but of falling off their horses. We on the other hand, with our feet firmly planted on the earth, can give much harder blows . . . and are much more likely to hit what we aim at. There is only one way in which cavalry have an advantage over us, and that is that it is safer for them to run away than it is for us.
(*The Persian Expedition*, III, 2,18–19 in *Anabasis*.)

The Spartan phalanx

The most disciplined and warlike of all the Greeks were the Spartans. Their phalanx was described by the Greek historian Plutarch (c AD46–c127):

Once their phalanx was marshalled together in sight of the enemy, the king sacrificed the customary she-goat . . . and ordered the pipers to play. . . . It was a sight at once solemn and terrifying to see them marching in step to the pipes, creating no gap in the phalanx . . . but approaching the confrontation calmly.
(Plutarch, *Life of Lycurgus*, XXII, 2–3.)

A Roman legionary

A Roman legionary was a full-time professional soldier. He joined up at about eighteen, and for the next twenty-five years the legion would be his home and family. Life was tough and pay was low. Only the poorest Romans were attracted by the security offered by being a soldier.

The legionary wore chest armour of overlapping plates, which allowed him to bend and move freely. He carried a curved shield made of wood and leather, two javelins for throwing, and a short sword for stabbing at close quarters. Much of his time would be spent drilling and marching with heavy equipment. It was important to keep the legionaries fit.

A legionary was a labourer as well as a fighter. At the end of each day's march, he had to help build a camp. He also quarried stone and built roads. In fact legionaries usually spent more time working on building projects than fighting.

The Romans believed that they had a right to rule other nations. They said that they brought peace and good government to the lands they conquered. They looked down on many of the people they fought as 'barbarians' (uncivilized people) and claimed that they were doing them a favour by giving them Roman civilization.

Wars brought Rome great wealth, in the form of captured slaves and taxes from the defeated people.

Roman soldiers bring a prisoner to their officer. Men, women and children prisoners were sold as slaves in the Empire's markets.

Caspian Sea

Boundary of the Empire in AD 117

Britain

Germany

Belgium

France

Atlantic
Ocean

Spain

Corsica

Sardinia

Rome

Italy

Sicily

Africa

Adriatic Sea

Greece

Black Sea

Armenia

Asia

Syria

Cyprus

Crete

Mediterranean Sea

Egypt

steel plate armour

A legionary on the march, weighed
down with weapons and tools.

pole for carrying
belongings

mess tin

food
bag

turf cutter

pick handle

water
bag

javelin – weighted
with a lead ball

sandals – the soles
are strengthened
with iron studs

Slave traders followed behind the battling legions buying up captives to provide the Romans with a huge, cheap labour force. Thanks to the wealth raised by warfare, the people of Rome did not have to pay any taxes themselves.

It was because of the army's discipline that the Romans were able to conquer their enemies. Most of Rome's enemies fought bravely, but as individual warriors. In contrast, the Roman soldiers fought together in tight formation, obeying battle commands given by trumpet signals which told them to face first one way then another. At another given trumpet signal, they could open their ranks to allow fresh troops to come to the front.

New recruits to the legion were drilled twice a day until they understood the trumpet signals. They learned to fight using weighted wooden swords and shields. To keep fit, they had to run and vault a wooden horse wearing full armour.

As well as a short sword, each legionary had a small dagger, worn on the left side of his belt.

Much of the time was spent marching. Each legionary would carry his armour, tools (such as an axe, saw and pick), a cooking pot, a sickle for reaping corn and enough food for three days. Most of this was carried on a pole over the soldier's shoulders. Every eight men would also have a mule, to carry their communal tent and two mill-stones for grinding corn.

Carrying their load, the legionaries could march 30 km each day and then build a camp for the night. Legionary camps were defended by an earth embankment and a deep ditch. For winter quarters and forts to defend the Roman Empire's frontiers the soldiers built permanent barracks.

Legionaries who showed cowardice or disobeyed orders were ruthlessly punished. If a soldier fell asleep on guard duty he would be beaten to death by his comrades, as he had risked their lives.

Roman standards
Each legion had its own battle standards on poles. They showed a silver or gold eagle as well as other symbols. These served as rallying points on the battlefield, but they also represented the honour of the legion and were treated as religious objects. They were kept in specially built temples in the camp where they were decorated with garlands. The greatest disgrace a legion could suffer was to lose its standards in battle.

A Roman legion
A Roman legion was made up of about 5,500 men, including clerks, surgeons and craftsmen – carpenters and blacksmiths. There would also be 120 horsemen, who acted as scouts and messengers. The fighting force was divided into ten battalions called cohorts, each containing about 480 men. A cohort was divided into six centuries, each commanded by an officer called a centurion. Every legion had a number and a name. This might be the name of the country where the legion was raised or it might be a nickname. The Twelfth Legion, for example, was called *Fulminata*, or 'lightning'. By AD 197 there were thirty-three legions in the Roman army – spread throughout the Empire.

A unit which refused to go into battle was punished with decimation: this meant that every tenth man, selected by drawing lots, would be flogged to death. But courage was rewarded. Soldiers were given medals and arm and neck bands for acts of bravery, such as saving another soldier's life. A legionary might also win promotion to the rank of officer or centurion. The most senior centurion's pay was more than sixteen times that of the lowest paid legionaries.

A Roman camp

A Roman camp was like a miniature town, with streets and a market place. It would always have the same layout and the soldiers would always pitch their tents in the same places. The Greek writer Polybius said that when a Roman army pitched camp after a day's march, it was as if it had returned home. It was hard work building the camp each day. But the advantage was that the soldiers felt safe and secure in otherwise hostile territory.

A Roman camp.

Watling Street, one of Britain's Roman roads.

Roman roads

The Romans built a huge network of very good roads throughout the Empire. The roads enabled the legions to move quickly from one place to another. From time to time peoples that the Romans had conquered tried to break free from the Empire. Such rebellions were easier to stop when the army could reach a trouble-spot rapidly.

A crusading knight

A crusade was a war fought in the name of the Christian religion against the followers of different religions. The most important crusades were fought between 1095 and 1300 against Muslims. Knights from all over Western Europe took part in these wars. Their purpose was to conquer Palestine, which Christians called the Holy Land.

The knights who went on crusades were members of the nobility. Only nobles could afford to buy armour and a *destrier*, a warhorse specially bred for strength and speed. From their childhood they had been trained to fight on horseback while wearing a heavy coat of mail. Fighting was the only skill they knew.

The knights' main tactic was a massed charge. A knight would ride with his feet stuck out straight in long stirrups, cradling a lance under his right arm. After a slow start, the horses would gather speed until they crashed into the enemy army. There was a tremendous impact – it was said that a mounted knight could bore a hole through a city's walls. Then the knights would draw their long swords for hand-to-hand fighting.

Knights who promised to go on a crusade had a long and difficult journey ahead of them. In the Middle Ages, ships were small, and most people were terrified of the sea. The land route to the Holy Land was even more dangerous, for much of it passed through Muslim territory. Once they had arrived in the East, the crusaders had to survive in a hostile land, far from home, where they were as likely to die from thirst and disease as to be killed in battle. But, despite all these risks, thousands of knights were eager to go on crusades.

Feudal society

European society in the Middle Ages was organized for war. Under the 'feudal system' all land was owned by the king, who parcelled it out among his great lords in exchange for their military services. In turn, they gave estates to knights who served them in wartime. Each knight would swear an oath of loyalty to his overlord. Loyalty and bravery were the greatest qualities a knight could have.

The stirrup

The knights' tactics were made possible by the stirrup. This was invented in China in the fourth century AD, and gradually spread westwards, reaching Europe in the eighth century. Stirrups gave the knight a secure seat on his horse. Without them, he would have been unable to charge with a lance – the impact of his blow would have knocked him off his horse. Thanks to the stirrup, horses dominated battles throughout the Middle Ages.

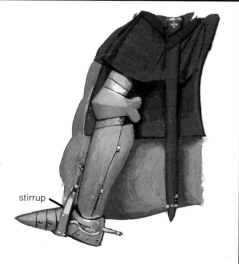

stirrup

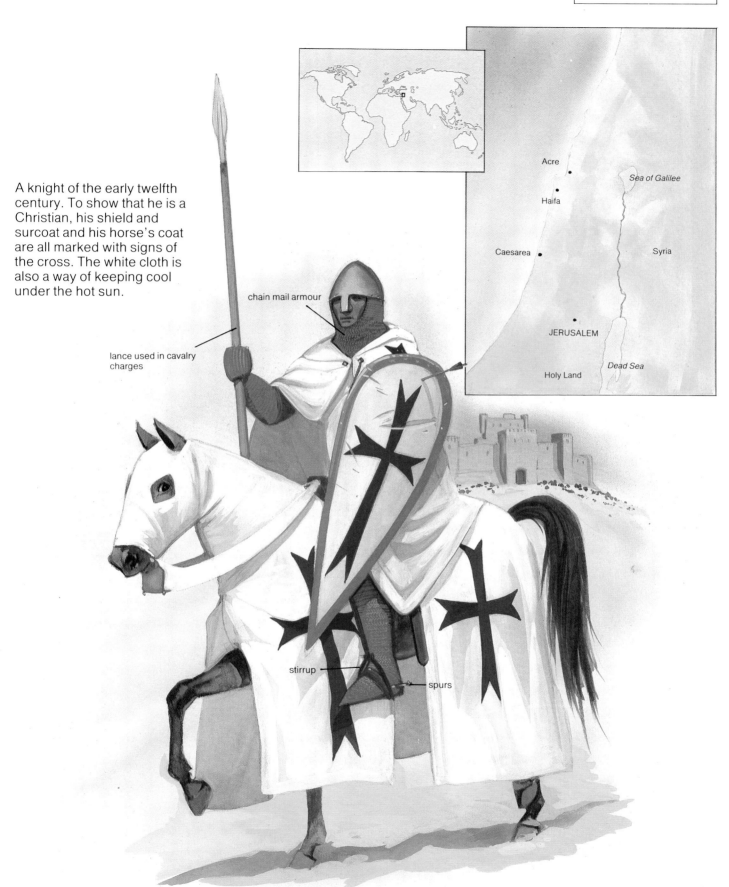

A knight of the early twelfth century. To show that he is a Christian, his shield and surcoat and his horse's coat are all marked with signs of the cross. The white cloth is also a way of keeping cool under the hot sun.

chain mail armour

lance used in cavalry charges

Acre

Sea of Galilee

Haifa

Caesarea

Syria

JERUSALEM

Dead Sea

Holy Land

stirrup

spurs

A crusading knight

Why did they go? Many of them hoped to make their fortune in the East by conquering new lands. It was also a chance to win fame and glory. But the most important motive was religious faith. The crusaders believed that Muslims were the enemies of God and that God wanted them to drive his enemies out of the Holy Land. The battle cry of the First Crusade was 'God

The lightly armed Muslims were no match for the knights in hand-to-hand combat.

wills it!' The knights believed they had God on their side, and they were sure they would win. But they also believed that if they died on the crusade, they would go straight to heaven. At a time when all Christians were scared of burning in hell, this was an important motive.

A glorious death
In a book addressed to the crusading knights, a French abbot called Bernard of Clairvaux wrote:
How glorious are the victors who return from battle! How blessed are the martyrs who die in battle! Rejoice, courageous athlete, if you live and conquer in the Lord, but glory the more if you die and are joined to the Lord. Life indeed is fruitful and victory glorious, but . . . death is better than either of these things.
(Bernard of Clairvaux, *On the New Knighthood* circa 1130.)

Above A wooden siege tower. Sometimes the crusaders were so short of timber that they had to break up their ships in order to build their siege towers.

Right The siege of Jerusalem, the Holy City, by the crusaders, from a 15th century manuscript.

When they arrived in the East, the crusaders found they had great difficulty in defeating the Muslims. Muslim cities and castles were more strongly defended than those of Europe, with thick stone walls and tall towers. The crusaders had to learn how to lay siege to a city using wooden towers and giant catapults. Much of their time was spent camped outside enemy cities, waiting to starve the defenders into surrender. Sieges could last months.

Even when they met the Muslims in the open, the knights found that their usual way of fighting did not always work. The Muslims were archers, who wore little armour and rode on small, swift horses. They kept at a safe distance from the knights, firing arrows at them. The Muslims rarely gave the knights a chance to launch one of their massed cavalry charges. They also had a favourite tactic of pretending to flee, in order to make the crusaders chase after them, only to lure them into an ambush.

The knights were more interested in showing off their personal bravery than in obeying orders, and so they were often drawn into the Muslims' ambushes.

Only the First Crusade of 1096–99 had any success: the crusaders set up four Christian states in the East. Once the Muslims stopped quarrelling amongst themselves and united, they slowly reconquered the crusader states.

Muslim tactics

A chaplain who took part in the Third Crusade (1189–92) complained: *The Turks, unlike our men, are not weighed down with armour, so they are able to advance more rapidly, and often inflict serious damage on our forces. When forcibly driven off they flee on very swift horses, the fastest in the world, like swallows for speed. Also they have a trick of halting in their flight when they see that their pursuers have given up the chase. An irritating fly, if you drive it off, will leave you, but when you stop, it returns. This is just like the Turk.* (Itinerarium regis Ricardi [anonymous chronicle of the Third Crusade] quoted in *Chronicles of the Crusades*, 1989, p.189.)

A Mongol horseman

Between 1200 and 1300, the Mongols conquered the greatest land empire in world history. Their armies fought in places as far apart as Japan and Poland, Palestine and Indonesia. They devastated whole countries, burning cities and massacring vast numbers of people.

A Mongol warrior fought, and often lived, on horseback. He would have learned to ride at the age of three, when his mother tied him to the saddle of one of the short, stocky Mongol horses. He became such a good horseman that he could sleep in the saddle if he had to. Each warrior took a number of horses with him, which he would ride in turn. Thanks to this system of remounts, Mongol armies could travel 200 km in two days.

The main Mongol weapon was the bow and arrow. With his feet in short stirrups, an archer could twist and turn in the saddle, firing arrows in all directions. He was dangerous even when fleeing. The Mongols also used heavy cavalrymen, who wore armour made from leather covered with thin metal strips. They were armed with swords and long lances, fitted with hooks for pulling other riders off their mounts.

The Mongols' homeland was the steppes, the vast grass-covered plains of Asia. This was a harsh terrain, bitterly cold and windy for most of the year. Here they lived as nomads, moving from place to place with their cattle and sheep, looking for fresh pastures, and following herds of deer which they hunted. The animals provided almost all their needs – food, drink, clothing and shelter. They slept in yurts, or tents, made from felt.

Life on horseback
The Italian traveller, Marco Polo, lived for many years among the Mongols. He wrote of them:
Of all men, they are the best able to bear hardship, and the cheapest to maintain and therefore the best fitted for conquering territory and overthrowing kingdoms. . . They can ride a good ten day's journey without provisions and without making a fire, living only on the blood of their horses; for every rider pierces a vein of his horse and drinks the blood.
(*The Travels of Marco Polo.*)

The Mongol hunt
Mongol warfare developed from hunting. A Mongol hunt was a huge operation, in which widely separated groups of horsemen would approach a herd of deer from different directions, riding silently so as not to alert the game. Similarly in war, Mongol armies would enter a country in different groups, communicating with smoke signals. As in a hunt, orders would be passed silently, using coloured flags and lanterns.

As well as hunting for food, the Mongols hunted with hawks for sport.

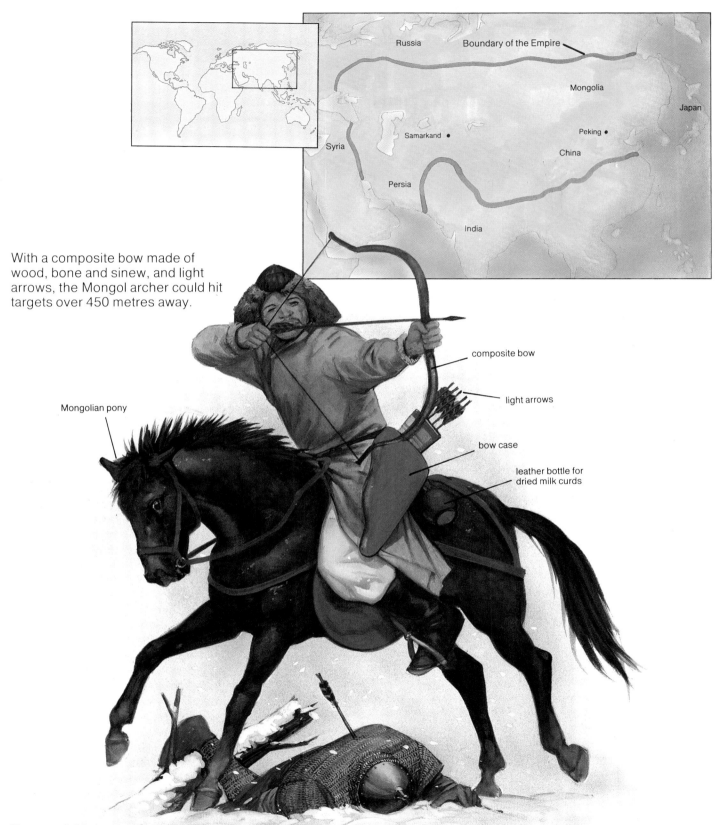

With a composite bow made of wood, bone and sinew, and light arrows, the Mongol archer could hit targets over 450 metres away.

Mongolian pony

composite bow

light arrows

bow case

leather bottle for dried milk curds

The tough Mongols were as happy campaigning in the cold of the Russian winter as in the heat of the Middle East. This light horseman is fighting in the snow of Russia (c 1223). Tied to his saddle is a leather bottle for dried milk curds – mixed with water to make a drink like yogurt.

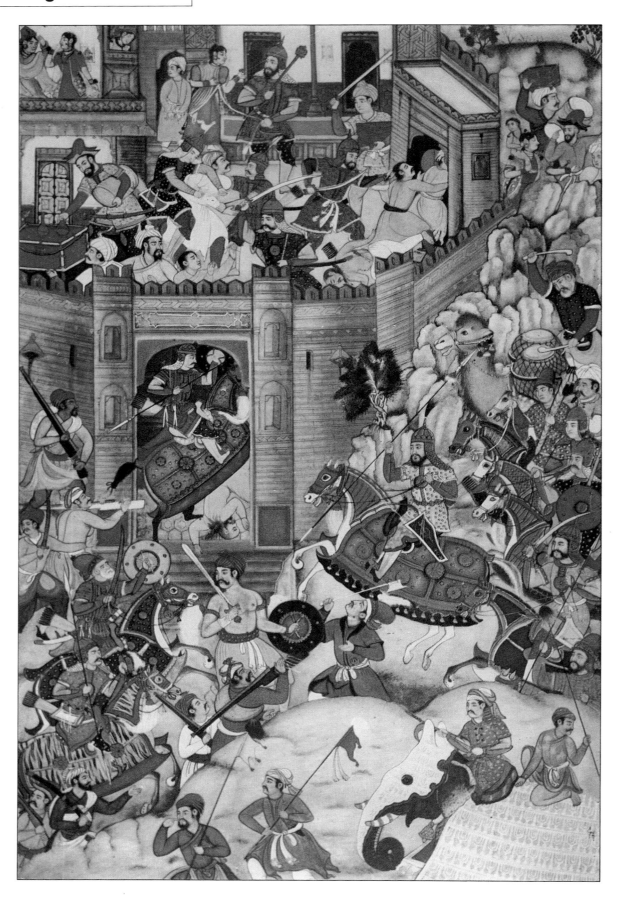

Left In this sixteenth century Persian painting, Genghis Khan sacks a Chinese city. The guns carried by some of the warriors belong to the sixteenth century.

Above the flat steppes, the sky seemed vast and mysterious. The Mongols worshipped the sky as a god, which they called *Tengri*, 'The Eternal Heaven.' They came to believe that they had been chosen as *Tengri*'s special servants.

Until the thirteenth century, the Mongols lived in many small tribes, each headed by a khan, or chief. But in 1206, they were united under the leadership of one man, Temujin. He took on the title Genghis Khan, which probably means 'universal ruler'. Genghis Khan and the rulers who followed him believed that they had a mission to conquer the world on behalf of their god, *Tengri*. They said that *Tengri* had given them all the world's empires, from sunrise to sunset.

Genghis Khan turned the different tribes into an efficiently organized army, split up into units of tens, hundreds and thousands. Each unit had its own commander. A Mongol warrior was assigned to his unit at the age of fourteen and, if he survived, he would remain in the same unit until he was sixty.

At first, the Mongols only fought in the open. But they soon learned to lay siege to walled cities, using catapults and battering rams. They would force large numbers of prisoners into the front lines during a siege, often making them dress as Mongol warriors. The idea was to exhaust the enemy by making them use their weapons against these prisoners, whose lives meant nothing to the Mongols.

Gunpowder

The Mongols may have been the first people to use gunpowder in warfare. They experimented with simple cannon – bamboo tubes which fired pellets to a distance of 200 m. Early guns were not very effective – they were just as likely to injure the people firing them as the enemy. Like the stirrup, gunpowder was a Chinese invention which changed the way that wars were fought.

Once a city was taken, all its inhabitants were usually killed. The Mongols would cut off the right ears of the corpses and collect them in sacks to be counted. After one battle, they were said to have collected nine sacks of ears. Then they would burn the city down.

It is hard to understand killing and destruction on such a scale. Some people think that the Mongols acted like this because they feared and hated walled cities. But the killing did have a practical use. As news of the massacres spread, people became so terrified that they would often surrender without a fight. The Mongols believed they were invincible thanks to their god *Tengri*. However, they lost their Empire when it became too huge to be ruled by one Khan.

Fear as a weapon

Fear was an important Mongol weapon, destroying people's will to fight back. The terror inspired by the Mongols was described by a Muslim historian, Ibn al-Athir, in 1231.

I have been told things that are hard to believe, so great was the terror of the people. It is said that a single Tartar (Mongol) horseman rode into a densely populated village and began killing the inhabitants one after another, without anyone trying to defend himself. . . . I have heard that one of them, having no weapon on him and wishing to kill someone whom he had taken prisoner, ordered the man to lie down on the ground, then went and fetched a sword and killed the wretch, who had not moved. (Ibn al-Athir *Kamil at-Tawarikh*.)

An Aztec warrior

The Aztecs of Mexico saw war as a religious duty. Its purpose was to capture prisoners to sacrifice to the gods, in particular to the war and sun god, Huitzilopochtli. They believed that if they failed to feed the gods with human blood, the sun would not rise and the world would be destroyed.

The aim of Aztec warfare was not to kill an enemy, but to take him prisoner so that he could be sacrificed in their temples. Killing an enemy in battle was seen as clumsy and wasteful. It was through capturing prisoners that a warrior gained respect.

Each Aztec warrior wore a tight-fitting suit of padded cotton, which had been stiffened by soaking in salt water. He carried a wooden shield and a *maquahuitl*, a wooden sword fitted with razor-sharp blades of obsidian (a type of volcanic rock). He went into battle with his face painted and his shield and clothes decorated with feathers. The most important warriors carried feather-decorated banners strapped to their backs so that their followers could recognize them. An Aztec army was a colourful and frightening sight.

The Aztecs needed a constant supply of people to sacrifice to their gods, and so they were almost always at war. Every male Aztec was trained to be a warrior. Soon after a boy

The Aztec gods, hungry for human blood, from a fourteenth century Mexican book painted on deerskin.

was born, he was handed a tiny bow and set of arrows. He would be taught to fight using wooden swords and shields. Each boy had his hair cut short apart from one long tuft of hair at the back. This would only be cut off when he had taken his first prisoner.

Tenochtitlan

Tlaxcala

Huexotzingo

Cholula

Gulf of Mexico

Pacific Ocean

Aztec Empire 1500

Area paying tribute to Aztecs

maquahuitl sword made with obsidian blades set in a wooden shaft

quetzal feathers

wooden shield decorated with feathers

jaguar skin

Battle

The Aztecs made a terrifying noise when they went into battle, blowing on conch shell horns and whistles, beating drums and yelling. They started the battle by firing arrows, javelins and stones at the enemy. Then the Aztec army would charge forward for hand-to-hand fighting, using their *maquahuitl* swords. The fighting usually ended when a chief was captured – his followers would take this as an unlucky sign and would flee.

It was through warfare that a man could rise in society. A man who captured four prisoners was given the title of *tequihua*, which means 'brave warrior'. He was allowed to wear his hair in a topknot together with luxurious clothes and jewellery, such as lip and nose plugs and earrings. Men who did not fight well were looked down on, even if they were of noble birth. They had to wear clothes made of rabbit skin like common peasants, and were not allowed to eat fine foods. Death was the penalty for people found wearing clothes to which they were not entitled.

Success in war brought the Aztecs a large empire, including 450 towns and 15 million people. Unlike the Romans, the Aztecs did not directly govern the people in their empire. Local chiefs were allowed to rule their own people. What the conquerors wanted was tribute, in the form of food (cocoa, maize, beans and fruit), precious stones, feathers and animal skins. Their home city, Tenochtitlan, had a huge population, possibly as many as 360,000 people in 1519 (at which time London had a population of only 40,000). Each year, the city received 52,000 tonnes of food. Without this tribute, the Aztecs would have starved.

For the defeated people, raising the annual tribute was a terrible burden. They hated and feared their conquerors. Sometimes they rebelled against them and then there would be another war, which the Aztecs almost always won.

Sacrifice

The Aztecs believed that it was an honour to be sacrificed to their gods. Each year, thousands of prisoners were led up the steps of the great temple of Huitzilopochtli. They were stretched out on a stone slab and their beating hearts were torn out by a priest using an obsidian knife. In one four-day celebration in 1487, 20,000 prisoners were said to have been killed.

A sacrificial knife with a carved eagle warrior on its handle, made in honour of the god of the rising Sun, Huitzilopochtli.

The War of the Flowers

As well as fighting wars of conquest, the Aztecs fought a ceremonial type of battle called the War of the Flowers. They would challenge the neighbouring peoples of Tlaxcala, Cholula and Huexotzingo to send their best warriors to fight them. The Aztecs did not want to conquer these neighbours, for then there could be no more wars against them. So the War of the Flowers provided victims to be sacrificed and served as a training ground for warriors.

Eagle and Jaguar warriors

The very best fighters were allowed to join special military orders – the eagle warriors and the jaguar warriors. Both had their own special uniforms. An eagle warrior wore a wooden helmet shaped like an eagle's head, with his face looking through the open beak. A jaguar warrior wore the skin of a jaguar over his padded cotton suit. The eagle warriors were specially devoted to the god Huitzilopochtli, while the jaguar warriors served Tezcatlipoca, god of the night sky.

In 1519–21, the Aztec Empire was finally conquered by a tiny force of Spaniards, led by Hernan Cortes. The Mexicans had never seen Europeans, horses or guns before. At first they thought the new arrivals were gods. Although the Spaniards were outnumbered, they were joined by several tribes who welcomed the chance to overthrow the Aztecs. The Spaniards were expert swordsmen. Their steel swords were much more effective than *maquahuitls*, for they could be used for stabbing as well as slashing. Unlike the

Part of a picture history of the Spanish conquest painted by their allies, the Tlaxcalans, whose warriors are shown in the foreground. This shows the Spaniards' horses and a fierce hunting dog – the Mexicans had never seen these animals before and found them terrifying.

Aztecs, they did not bother with taking prisoners but tried to kill as many people as possible in each battle.

A Prussian musketeer

The army of Frederick the Great, King of Prussia, was made up of peasant soldiers commanded by noble officers. It seemed natural to the Prussians that the army came from these two classes; the peasants had grown up obeying orders from the nobles on their country estates.

The soldiers wore identical uniforms and spent much of their time drilling – learning to march in step and to load and fire their muskets at the same time. In battle, they would advance close together in three rows to the beat of a drum. When they were near enough to the enemy, they would fire a volley (a round of fire) and then charge with their bayonets.

The complicated stages of musket drill. If the soldiers fired at the wrong time, they were likely to shoot each other.

Living machines
Dr J Moore, an English visitor to Prussia in the 1780s, described the army's discipline: *As to the common men, the idea of Prussian discipline is to turn them . . . into machines; be directed solely by their officers; that they may have such a . . . dread of those officers as destroys all fear of the enemy; and that they may move forward when ordered, without more concern than the flintlocks they carry. (A View of Society and Manners in France, Switzerland and Germany Vol II, 1789.)*

zieht ihn rauß;   bringt ihn an seinen Orth.   bringt das Gewehr für euch.   Schuldert euer Gewehr.   Præsentirt das Gewehr.   Das Gewehr hoch.

Sweden

Denmark

North Sea

East Prussia

West Prussia

German states

Silesia 1742

Poland

Austrian territory

France

Prussian territory 1740

Lands conquererd
by Frederick the Great

Austrian territory

Swedish territory

tricorne felt hat

musket

private

officer

sword/bayonet in
sheath

A musketeer practises the movements of drill, watched over by an officer holding a stick. The stick is used to strike the soldier whenever he makes a mistake.

Officers beat their soldiers for the slightest offence. One of Frederick's favourite sayings was that a common soldier should fear his officers more than the enemy. This harshness was necessary to make the troops march towards the enemy's cannon and to make them keep marching even when their comrades were being killed around them. 'If my soldiers began to think,' said Frederick, 'no one would remain in the ranks.'

In the eighteenth century, Germany did not exist as a single country. The German-speaking people belonged to around 350 different states, some of them only a few hectares in size. Prussia was just one of these many states. It was a small, poor country, surrounded by powerful neighbours.

Frederick the Great, who ruled Prussia from 1740 to 1786, believed that his kingdom had to conquer neighbouring territory in order to survive. He launched a series of wars against the Austrians, the French, the Swedes and the Russians. Thanks to the discipline of his troops, he usually won.

Soon after Frederick came to the throne, he raised the

Frederick directing his troops at the Battle of Kolin in 1757 does not notice the dead beneath his horse's hooves.

army's strength from 90,000 to 150,000 men. This made it the fourth largest army in Europe, incredible for a country with only 2.5 million people. Mirabeau, the French politician, said: 'Most states have an army. Prussia is the only case of an army having a state.'

Most of the soldiers were poor Prussian peasants.

Standing armies

In a letter of 1770, Frederick defended the use of full-time soldiers in standing armies:

Today, at the first trumpet blast, neither the farmer, the manufacturer, the lawyer, nor the scholar, are diverted from their work; they continue peacefully to pursue their normal occupations. . . . In former times, at the first alarm, troops were hastily levied and everyone became a soldier . . . the fields lay fallow, the professions languished, and the soldiers, ill-paid . . . ill-disciplined, lived only by looting. . . . All that has greatly changed. (Letter to d'Alembert, 18 October 1770.)

Training to the whip

The French writer, Voltaire, spent years at the Prussian court. In this extract from his novel *Candide* (1759), the hero has just been seized by a press-gang:

They clapped him into irons and hauled him off to barracks. There he was taught 'right turn', 'left turn', and 'quick march', 'slope arms' and 'order arms', how to aim and how to fire, and was given thirty strokes of the 'cat o' nine tails'. Next day his performance on parade was a little better, and he was given only twenty strokes. The following day he received a mere ten and was thought a marvel by his comrades. (*Candide*, Chapter II.)

They were conscripted for a limited period. But almost a third of the army was made up of foreigners, mercenaries or people who had been kidnapped by Frederick's press-gangs. During a campaign, the Prussians also forced enemy deserters and prisoners of war into the ranks. After 1780, military service was made a punishment for convicted criminals.

With so many unwilling soldiers, the army was always threatened by desertion. Many of the soldiers would run away at the first opportunity. While fighting Austria in 1777–78, the Prussians lost 3,500 men in battle but 16,000 by desertion. Frederick advised his officers that they were never to camp near a forest, never to march or attack by night and not to tell the troops in what direction they would march the next day. It was said that one half of Frederick's army was needed to guard and whip the other half.

In previous centuries armies had been allowed to live off the country. But Frederick could not trust his troops to forage freely. Instead, they had to be kept supplied by the government. Magazines (supply depots) were set up along Prussia's borders and stocked with food. Armies could not move more than five days' march from any magazine.

The eighteenth century has been described as a time of 'limited warfare'. Wars had to be short, for it was expensive and difficult to keep an army in the field. As a result, civilians were spared many of the horrors which previously came from war. There was little looting or destruction of civilian property. Poor people suffered, for they had to fight but the middle classes were hardly affected by war.

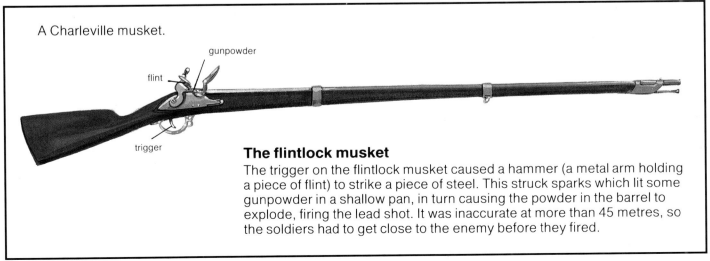

A Charleville musket.

gunpowder

flint

trigger

The flintlock musket

The trigger on the flintlock musket caused a hammer (a metal arm holding a piece of flint) to strike a piece of steel. This struck sparks which lit some gunpowder in a shallow pan, in turn causing the powder in the barrel to explode, firing the lead shot. It was inaccurate at more than 45 metres, so the soldiers had to get close to the enemy before they fired.

A soldier in the American Civil War

A civil war is a conflict between people of the same nation. The American Civil War of 1861–65 was fought between the southern states, who wanted to split away from the American Union and form their own Confederacy, and the northern states, who fought to preserve the Union.

The soldiers of both armies had much in common. Many were farmers but the rest came from all areas of civilian life. Most had never been away from home before. They joined up thinking that the war would be a great adventure.

We know more about the ordinary soldiers of this war than any previous one. It was the first war to be widely photographed.

The dead lie on the battlefield of Antietam, 17 September 1862. Photographs like this made civilians aware for the first time of the horrors of war.

Into battle

After the battle of Antietam in September 1862, sixteen-year-old Union Private William Brierley wrote to his father: *I have seen pictures of battles – they would all be in a line, all standing in a nice level field fighting, a number of ladies taking care of the wounded, etc. But it isn't so . . . We rushed onto them every man for himself – all loading and firing as fast as he could see a rebel to shoot at. The firing increased tenfold until it sounded like the rolls of thunder – and all the time every man shouting as loud as he could.* (Quoted in *The Life of Billy Yank. The Common Soldier of the Union*, 1962, pp. 78, 84.)

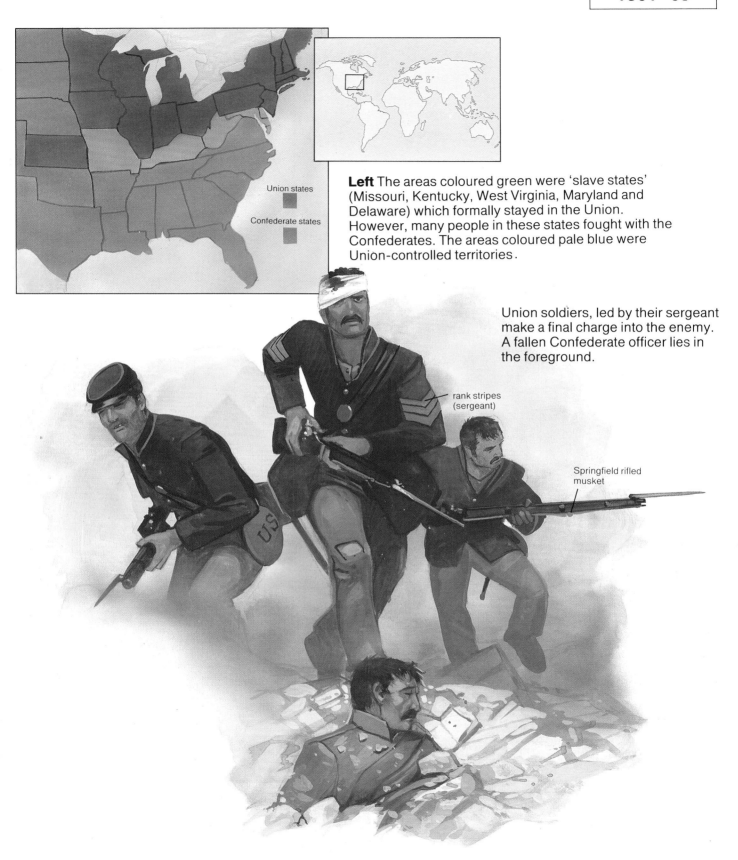

Union states

Confederate states

Left The areas coloured green were 'slave states' (Missouri, Kentucky, West Virginia, Maryland and Delaware) which formally stayed in the Union. However, many people in these states fought with the Confederates. The areas coloured pale blue were Union-controlled territories.

Union soldiers, led by their sergeant make a final charge into the enemy. A fallen Confederate officer lies in the foreground.

rank stripes (sergeant)

Springfield rifled musket

Photographers followed the armies, taking portraits of the soldiers for them to send home to their families. They also visited the battlefields, photographing the dead. It was the first war in which large numbers of soldiers were able to read and write. They spent many of the long, boring hours in camp writing letters to their families. For the first time, we hear the voice of the ordinary soldier, describing what it was like to go into battle.

The American Civil War has often been described as the first modern war. Unlike the 'limited warfare' fought by Frederick the Great, it was a total war – it affected everyone. Each side eventually introduced conscription, calling up all fit young men. Almost three million soldiers took part. The industries of both sides switched to producing weapons and other war materials. The final victory, which went to the Union, depended on factory workers as much as soldiers.

The cause of the war was the southerners' fear that the Union Government intended to outlaw slavery; their economy depended on the black slaves who worked on the cotton plantations. But for the majority of the ordinary

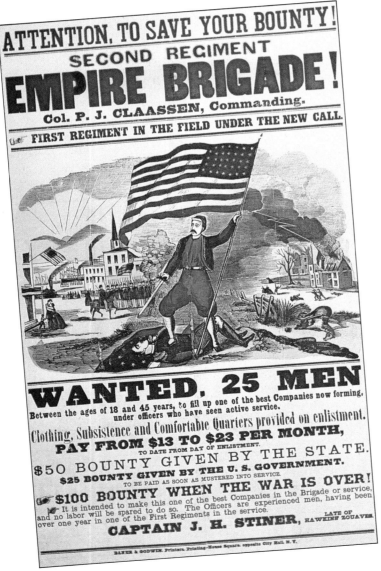

This Union recruiting poster promises a 'bounty', or special payment, to volunteers. Money was always an important motive for joining up – the war took place at a time of widespread unemployment.

War against civilians

In November 1864, the Union General William Sherman led his army south from Atlanta to the sea, burning everything in his path. The aim was to wreck the South's economy and destroy civilian morale. People complained that this was breaking all the rules of war. Sherman justified his tactics in these words:
War is cruelty. There is no use trying to reform it. The crueller it is, the sooner it will be over.
(Quoted in *Sherman, Fighting Prophet*, 1932, p. 330.)

The Springfield rifle could fire ten times in five minutes.

soldiers, slavery was not an issue. Most of the southern soldiers did not own slaves; they were fighting simply out of loyalty to their home states.

The soldiers were armed with the new rifled-musket, a gun with a spiral groove inside its barrel. This spun the bullet as it was fired, giving it much greater accuracy and range. They also began to use repeating rifles, which could fire shot after shot without reloading. At the battle of Shiloh, in 1862, one Confederate said that if he had held up a bucket, it would have filled immediately with bullets.

Despite the new weapons, the generals still expected the infantry to charge in a massed attack, like the Prussian musketeers of the eighteenth century. As a result, civil war battles were the bloodiest that had ever been seen. In one battle, at Cold Harbor, in June 1864, 7,000 men fell in the first 20 minutes.

The new weapons caused horrifying injuries. Medical methods were primitive and often did more harm than good.

Stomach and chest wounds were almost always fatal. Soldiers wounded in the legs or arms would usually have to have them amputated (cut off) to prevent gangrene setting in. But the surgeons used dirty instruments, and so gangrene and tetanus would often kill the patient anyway. Yet many did survive; in the first year after the war, a fifth of the Mississippi state budget was spent on artificial limbs for returning soldiers.

The greatest killer was not enemy gunfire, but disease. For every soldier killed in battle, two others died of sickness. In the winter the soldiers died from pneumonia and in the summer from typhoid and malaria. Living in close contact with large numbers of other people, the soldiers were exposed to a host of diseases that were new to them – measles, chicken pox, scarlet fever and mumps. These illnesses, mild in

childhood, were often fatal to adults. The most common complaint was diarrhoea, caused by drinking dirty water polluted by the camp latrines. This complaint, which the soldiers nicknamed the 'Virginia Quickstep', proved to be the single greatest cause of death in the war.

Meeting the enemy

Soldiers from the two sides often organized informal truces so that they could trade – the southerners wanted coffee, which the northerners had, while the northerners wanted the southerners' tobacco. After one meeting, a Union soldier wrote:

It seems too bad that we have to fight men that we like . . . Now these southern soldiers seem just like our own boys. They talk about . . . their mothers and fathers and their sweethearts just as we do.
(Quoted in *The Life of Billy Yank, The Common Soldier of the Union*, 1962, p. 356.)

A British soldier in the Somme

The First World War was fought on the Western Front by two vast armies facing each other from opposing lines of trenches, from the North Sea to the Swiss border. On one side were the French, British and British Empire forces, later joined by the Americans; facing them was the German Army. Each side had a strong defensive position, protected by barbed wire and machine guns. Between the opposing lines of trenches lay no-man's land, a stretch of mud and shell craters.

In the summer of 1916, the British launched a major attack near the Somme river in France. It began with a week-long artillery bombardment on the German trenches. This was supposed to cut the Germans' barbed wire and destroy their artillery and machine guns. Then the British soldiers ('Tommies') were ordered to fix their bayonets and go 'over the top'. They expected to walk unopposed across no-man's-land.

However, unknown to the British, the Germans had been able to shelter throughout the bombardment in deep dug-outs. They knew as soon as the bombardment ended that the British were about to attack. So they raced to the surface, set up their machine guns and waited for the advancing lines to come within range.

On the first day of the Battle of the Somme, 21,000 British soldiers were killed and 39,000 were wounded, mown down by the German machine guns. Despite this terrible slaughter, the battle was to continue for four months. It would cost 420,000 British casualties.

Canadian machine gunners set up machine guns in water-filled shell holes. They have put down tarpaulins in an attempt to keep dry.

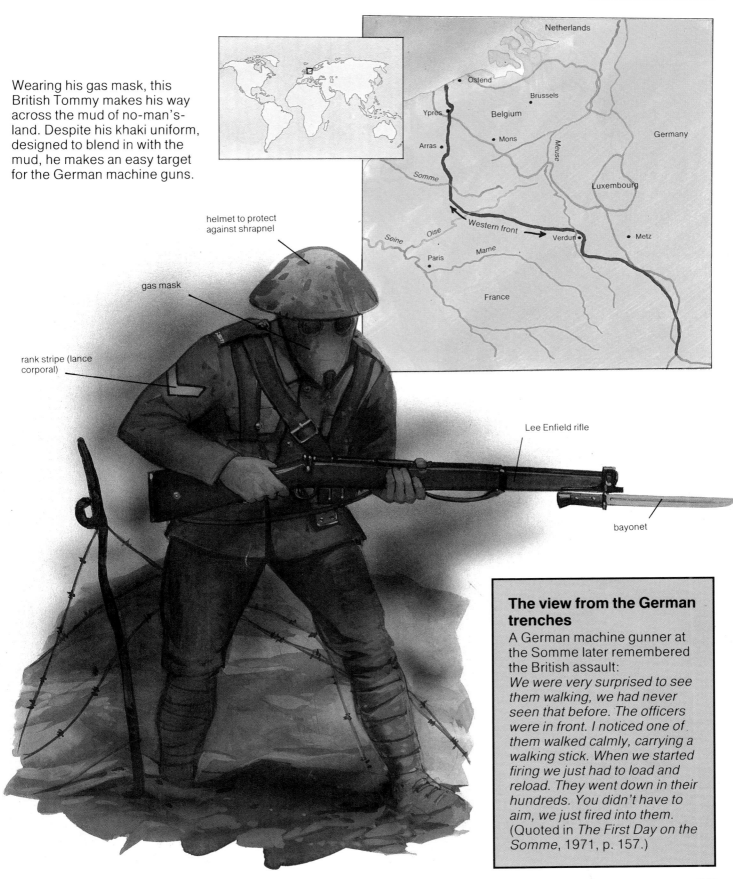

Wearing his gas mask, this British Tommy makes his way across the mud of no-man's-land. Despite his khaki uniform, designed to blend in with the mud, he makes an easy target for the German machine guns.

helmet to protect against shrapnel

gas mask

rank stripe (lance corporal)

Lee Enfield rifle

bayonet

The view from the German trenches

A German machine gunner at the Somme later remembered the British assault:
We were very surprised to see them walking, we had never seen that before. The officers were in front. I noticed one of them walked calmly, carrying a walking stick. When we started firing we just had to load and reload. They went down in their hundreds. You didn't have to aim, we just fired into them.
(Quoted in *The First Day on the Somme*, 1971, p. 157.)

Map labels: Netherlands, Ostend, Brussels, Ypres, Belgium, Germany, Arras, Mons, Meuse, Somme, Luxembourg, Seine, Oise, Western front, Verdun, Metz, Paris, Marne, France

At the start of the First World War, the British had a standing army of only 100,000 men. In order to raise troops, the Government called for volunteers. They were helped by British newspapers, which mounted a hate campaign against the enemy. Songs and posters urged all men to join up; anyone who refused was made to feel cowardly and unpatriotic. The recruiting campaign was a great success. By 1916, three million men had volunteered.

Many people thought the war would be over quickly and they were eager to get to the front before it finished. But, as the casualties of trench warfare mounted, it became clear that the war would be a long one. There would be no decisive military victory. It had become a war of attrition – the gradual wearing down of the enemy. Victory would go to the side which could outlast its opponent. In such a war, even three million men were not enough. In 1916, the British government used conscription, calling up all able-bodied men between the ages of eighteen and forty-one.

The Countess of Athlone (left) in uniform in the Women's Transport Service. Women, as well as men, were eager to help the war effort.

Life was terrible in the trenches. The soldiers were often up to their knees in rain-water. As a result, many of them suffered from 'trench foot' – caused by going to sleep with tight boots and wet feet. Soldiers with trench foot often lost their toes. Dirty food and water led to the outbreak of cholera and typhus. In the winter, the men suffered from exposure and frostbite. Their bodies and clothes were covered with lice. The trenches swarmed with rats which ate the dead and attacked sleeping and wounded soldiers.

There was a constant risk of death from an enemy sniper or shell. Both sides used poisonous mustard gas which caused terrible burns and blindness.

At the shout of 'gas!', all the men would have to pull on their protective masks as quickly as possible.

What every soldier dreaded was the order to go 'over the top' and attack the German trenches. Before an assault, the men would be issued with rum to give them courage. Then each platoon commander would blow his whistle, signalling the men to climb their ladders and leap into no-man's-land. Sometimes officers had to drive their men forward at gun point. 'Battle police' patrolled the trenches, making sure that no one was hiding when an attack was in progress.

By the end of the battle of the Somme, in November 1916, only a few kilometres of German-held territory had been captured at a terrible cost in Allied lives.

Many soldiers hoped for a 'cushy' – a minor wound which would take them home honourably. Almost four thousand men were tried for 'self-inflicted wounds' – they preferred to shoot off their own toes or fingers rather than go into battle.

Command from the rear
The generals who ordered the battles of trench warfare were usually far behind their own lines, and often out of touch with conditions at the front. The British troops made up a song about this:
Forward Joe Soap's Army, marching without fear
With our own commander, safely in the rear.
He boasts and strikes from morn till night and thinks he's very brave,
But the men who really do the job are dead and in their grave.
(Quoted in *Contemporary Accounts of the First World War*, 1981, p. 21.)

The moment of going 'over the top', captured by a photographer. In a few seconds, these men will be exposed to the German machine guns.

A soldier in the Red Army

The Second World War (1939–45) was a people's war; a war which affected civilians just as much as soldiers. The soldiers themselves were almost all conscripted civilians rather than professionals. With the introduction of a new weapon, the bomber plane, civilians suffered just as much as those in uniform. Of the war's estimated 45 million dead, 30 million were civilians; and within this group, 20 million, or two-thirds were citizens of the Soviet Union.

Unlike the stalemate of trench warfare, this was a war of rapid movement. The Germans pioneered a new way of fighting, using surprise attacks by columns of tanks supported by bomber planes. It was called blitzkrieg, German for 'lightning war'.

Blitzkrieg brought Germany a series of swift, easy victories. Much of Western Europe was conquered in campaigns lasting only a few weeks. When Germany invaded the Soviet Union, in June 1941, it looked as if the Red Army would be beaten just as quickly. The opening months of the invasion brought nothing but German victories. But the vast Soviet Union had almost unlimited reserves of people. Everyone was mobilized in the effort to win what the Soviets called 'The Great Patriotic War'.

The German soldiers (seen here in 1941) were not prepared for the bitter cold of the Russian winter.

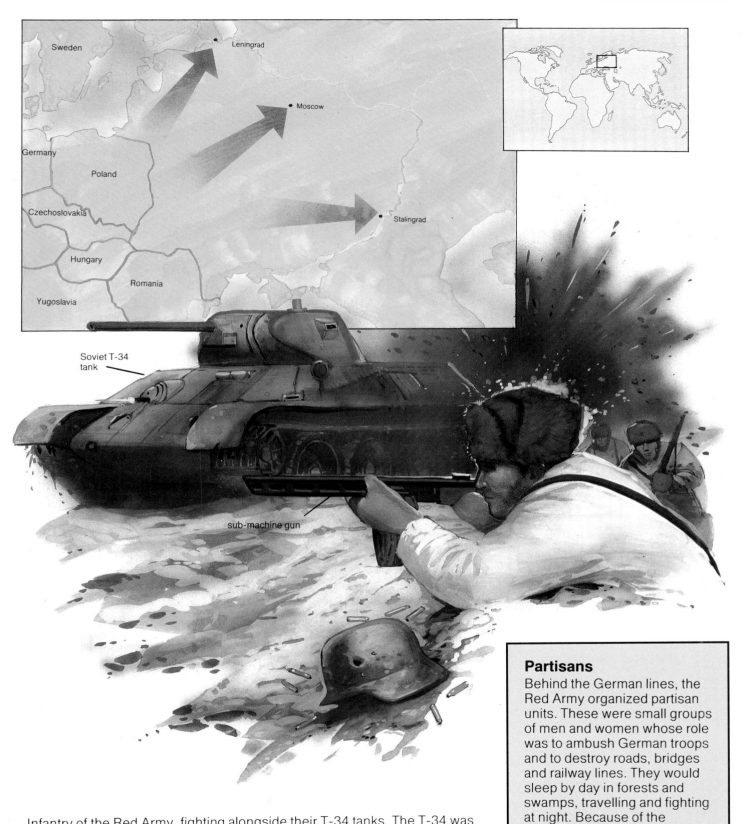

Soviet T-34
tank

sub-machine gun

Infantry of the Red Army, fighting alongside their T-34 tanks. The T-34 was the best designed tank of the war. It broke down less often than the German tanks, had a greater range of fire and its slanted turret could usually shrug off anti-tank missiles.

Partisans

Behind the German lines, the Red Army organized partisan units. These were small groups of men and women whose role was to ambush German troops and to destroy roads, bridges and railway lines. They would sleep by day in forests and swamps, travelling and fighting at night. Because of the partisans, the German soldiers could never feel safe.

The German campaign in the Soviet Union caused the hardest fighting of the Second World War. The German leader, Adolf Hitler, said that it was a 'war of extermination' against the Soviet people. Hitler believed that the Germans were the 'master race' and had the right to rule or destroy other races. Special units followed the advancing German armies, massacring Jews, Gypsies and Soviet officials. The rest of the Soviet population, Hitler planned, would work as slaves for their new masters.

Both sides saw the war as a life or death struggle. In the opening months, the Soviet Union met the invasion with a 'scorched earth' policy. Everything that might be of use to the Germans was destroyed. Everything that could be moved was loaded on trains and sent to the East. Whole factories were dismantled and rebuilt out of range of the enemy bombers.

German and Soviet soldiers were expected to fight to the death rather than surrender. Prisoners were badly treated by both sides, left to starve or used as slave labour in terrible conditions. Few survived to return home after the war.

The soldiers of both sides were trained to fear their officers more than the enemy. Behind each advancing army, there were secret police units, whose role was to make sure that soldiers obeyed orders. The Germans shot 15,000 of their own men for disobedience, cowardice or desertion. On the Soviet side, officers as well as ordinary soldiers were shot for failure. As a result, generals preferred to send troops to certain death rather than admit defeat.

The Red Army had millions of men and women at its disposal and so it could afford to waste soldiers' lives. Sometimes infantry

Soviet troops in Stalingrad in November 1942. Every street was fought for in a battle lasting from the summer of 1942 to February 1943.

The battle for Stalingrad

A German officer wrote:
Imagine Stalingrad, eighty days and eighty nights of hand-to-hand struggles. The street is no longer measured by metres but by corpses . . . when night arrives, the dogs plunge into the [river] Volga and swim desperately to gain the other bank. Animals flee this hell; the hardest stones cannot bear it for long; only men endure. (Quoted in *Hitler as Military Commander*, 1971, p. 165.)

Two Red Army soldiers were interviewed by a Western journalist at the end of the battle. The first describes his German opponents:
In these last weeks, they hated coming out into the open; they can't stand the cold . . . Filthy, dirty; you wouldn't believe in what filth they lived there. Scared of the cold and scared of our snipers . . . Funny blokes really. Coming to conquer Stalingrad wearing patent leather shoes. Thought it would be a joy-ride.

There's nothing left of Stalingrad; not a thing. If I had any say in the matter, I'd rebuild Stalingrad somewhere else; it would save a lot of trouble. And I'd leave this place as a museum.
(Quoted in *Russia at War 1941–5*, 1964.)

A Soviet woman pilot is congratulated after returning from a successful night raid.

Women soldiers

Women were vitally important to the Soviet war effort. Half of the front-line doctors and surgeons, and almost all the stretcher-bearers and nurses were women. In addition, some 800,000 women enlisted in the Red Army as soldiers. They served in mixed as well as all-women units, as tank crew members, machine gunners, snipers, dispatch riders and in the crews of the bomber planes.

units were sent across minefields to clear the way for the tanks – for the war effort, machines were often worth more than people.

The turning point of the war was the Battle of Stalingrad, which lasted from 23 August, 1942 to 2 February, 1943. This was a desperate battle for the control of the city. By November, when Stalingrad was little more than rubble, the Germans had almost won. But on 19 November, the Soviets launched a huge counter-attack, surrounding the city and trapping 300,000 German soldiers in its ruins. For over two months, the trapped German Army fought on, in the freezing cold with few supplies. The following February, the starving survivors finally surrendered.

After Stalingrad, the Germans were slowly driven back by the Red Army. But they continued to fight fiercely for another two years, as Hitler sent more and more soldiers to the East. The final Soviet victory over the Germans came with the fall of Berlin in May 1945. It marked the beginning of a new era for the Soviet Union as a world superpower.

A soldier in the Gulf War

Between January and March 1991, a war was fought over the tiny state of Kuwait in the Arabian Gulf. On one side was Iraq, which had invaded Kuwait in August 1990. Facing the Iraqi Army were soldiers from seventeen different countries (the Allies), the majority from the USA, Saudi Arabia, Egypt, Britain and France. Their aim was to make the Iraqis leave Kuwait. The Allied forces were fighting on behalf of the United Nations (UN), an international organization set up at the end of the Second World War to promote peace.

The rival armies were very different in character. While the Iraqis were mainly poorly trained conscripts, most of the Allied forces were full-time professional soldiers, people who had chosen the Army as a career. Many had spent years doing military exercises, and fighting mock battles. Yet the majority had not seen real combat before. This was the chance to put their training into practice.

The soldiers spent most of their time waiting. The UN had given the Iraqis a deadline, 15 January, to leave Kuwait. The soldiers of both sides knew that the war would begin on this date if the Iraqi leader, Saddam Hussein, did not back down. While the Allied soldiers waited to be sent into battle, the Iraqis waited to be attacked.

US infantry soldiers spent weeks training, waiting to be sent into battle.

The air war

The war began on 15 January with the biggest air raid in history. In the first 48 hours, the allies flew 2,107 missions over Iraq, bombing air fields, power stations and bridges.

After his first night bombing raid over Baghdad, British Flight Lieutenant Ian Long spoke to the news cameras: *It was the most scary thing I have ever done in my life. We went in low over the target – as low as we dared. We dropped the bombs and ran like hell. It was absolutely terrifying. We were frightened of failure and frightened of dying.* (*The Sunday Times*, 20 Jan., 1991.)

This US marine's bulky pack holds 27kg of equipment, including protective clothing to be worn in case of an attack by chemical or biological weapons.

27kg pack

Kevlar helmet

water bottle

entrenching tool

assault rifle with special sights for seeing targets at night

Waiting for the ground war

By February the ground forces knew that they would soon be sent into action. One Scots Guards soldier described his feelings:

When we first came, we never thought it would be war. Then we thought the air force would pound them into surrender. Then we thought Saddam would pull out. Now we all know that it is actually going to happen, and we are all scared. But we'll do the job all right. We've been trained for it for years; now it's for real.

A US soldier said:

It's considered common courtesy not to talk about how scared you are.

Another added:

It's better not to think about it anyway. That may sound brainless, but if you thought about it, you couldn't do it, and somebody has to do it.

(*Sunday Times*, Insight Team, 3 February, 1991. © Times Newspapers Ltd, 1991.)

War language

Throughout the war, the US Army gave daily press conferences to explain what was happening. They used their own words to describe events that might be unpopular. For example, enemy soldiers were not killed but 'taken out'; the word 'kill' was used only to refer to destroying machines; tanks were 'killed'. Civilian casualties were described as 'collateral damage'.

From the start of the Gulf War, everything went the Allies' way. The months leading up to the UN deadline allowed them to plan their offensive and get all their forces into position. Through spy planes and satellites, they were able to take detailed photographs of Iraqi troop positions and decide where to aim their bombs.

The Allies had all kinds of new weapons using the latest technology. For example, Allied troops had heat scanners which allowed them to spot Iraqi vehicles at night. They also had the latest navigation equipment allowing them to move rapidly across the desert without risk of getting lost.

When the air attack began, the Allied bombers met with little resistance. The Iraqi Air Force commanders, after seeing the first planes they sent out shot down, ordered pilots to fly their aircraft to Iran so they could not be destroyed by the Allies.

Unable to use aircraft, the Iraqis fired Scud missiles at the Allies in Saudi Arabia, and at civilian targets in Israel. Allied military officials warned that the Scud missiles could release

The controls of a Patriot missile system. The computer works out the direction and speed of an incoming missile and tells the operator exactly when to fire.

chemicals (such as mustard gas, which burns the skin and lungs, and nerve gas, which causes fits). But in fact all of the Scud missiles fired by Iraq carried explosives, not chemicals. With some exceptions, most of the Scuds either missed their targets or were shot down by US Patriot missiles, which use the latest technology to track and hit enemy missiles.

Pictures of the conflict were soon being beamed to televisions around the world. Every night, television viewers were shown Allied military films of precision bombing

by computer-guided missiles and bombs. These were described as 'surgical strikes': through pinpoint accuracy, the Allies claimed to be able to hit military targets without killing civilians. However, most of the bombs dropped on Iraq were not so precise and civilian targets were hit. The Iraqi capital, Baghdad, a city with 4 million inhabitants, was left without electricity, running water or working sewers.

On 24 February, after almost six weeks of bombing Iraq from the air, the Allies launched their ground attack. Massive numbers of tanks and armoured troop carriers swept across the desert into Kuwait and southern

Iraq. Iraq's demoralized troops offered almost no resistance, allowing Allied tanks and troops to pass through Iraqi defences. Kuwait City was recaptured by US, Egyptian and Saudi troops on 27 February. Meanwhile, Allied aircraft attacked Iraqi tanks trying to flee. By the time Iraq surrendered (on 3 March), more than 3,000 tanks had been destroyed.

Unlike soldiers in earlier wars and their Iraqi opponents, the Allied soldiers in the Gulf War were far from being 'cannon fodder'. They were all highly trained professionals, each carrying weapons and equipment costing thousands of pounds. Sealed inside armoured troop carriers, most of them saw the enemy they were fighting through television cameras – either those of news reporters or spy planes. Few saw Iraqi soldiers in person.

The Gulf War soldier had little in common with the part-time hoplite of Ancient Greece who fought his enemy hand-to-hand. In 1991, war seemed to have become, for the victorious soldier, a hi-tech 'game' with no blood or corpses. For a soldier on

Iraqi prisoners guarded by Saudi soldiers. By the end of the ground war, 175,000 Iraqis had surrendered.

the other side it had become a nightmare in which an enemy he could not see dropped 'smart' bombs which he could not dodge.

Gulf War casualties
Less than 200 Allied soldiers were killed, some of them by 'friendly fire' from their own side. It is not clear how many Iraqis were killed. Altogether Allied bombers flew 110,000 missions against Iraq. Estimates for the number of Iraqi casualties range between 20,000 and over 100,000.

Glossary

Ambush A surprise attack on the enemy from a hidden position.
Barracks A building used by soldiers as a base.
Bayonet A stabbing instrument fixed to a gun.
Campaign A period of sustained attack on the enemy.
Cat-o'-nine-tails A kind of whip with nine knotted strips of leather.
Cavalry Soldiers on horseback.
Civilian A person not serving in the armed forces.
Conscripted Called up and forced to join the army.
Felt Material made with matted wool.
Flintlock A gun with a flint used to fire it.
Gangrene A disease where a part of the body decays because the blood supply to it has been cut off. If gangrene has set in the infected part of the body must be removed in order to stop the infection spreading.
Herald An official messenger, who is sent to announce news.
Infantry Foot soldiers.
Invincible Unbeatable.
Javelin A light throwing spear.
Latrine Temporary toilet dug in an army camp.
Looting Stealing property from buildings damaged in war or riots.
Mercenary A soldier willing to fight for any army that hires him or her.
Patriotism The loyal support of one's own country.
Press-gang A group of soldiers who force unwilling civilians to join up.
Tribute A forced payment or contribution of goods to the ruler of a country.

Further reading

GENERAL BOOKS
Embleton, G A, *Warfare in History* (Wayland, 1984)
Windrow, Martin and Hook, Richard, *The Footsoldier* (Oxford University Press, 1982)

BOOKS ON PARTICULAR PERIODS
Burrell, Roy, *The Greeks* (Oxford University Press, 1989)
Powell, Anton, *The Greek World* (Kingfisher, 1987 (reprinted 1991))

Connolly, Peter, *The Legionary* (Oxford University Press, 1991)
Connolly, Peter, *The Roman Fort* (Oxford University Press, 1991)
Windrow, Martin, *The Roman Legionary* (Franklin Watts, 1984)
Chrisp, Peter, *The Crusades* (Wayland, 1992)
Ross, Stewart, *A Crusading Knight* (Wayland, 1986)
Langley, Andrew, *Genghis Khan and the Mongols* (Wayland, 1987)

Crosher, Judith, *The Aztecs* (Macdonald Educational, 1976 (reprinted 1985))
Steel, Anne, *An Aztec Warrior* (Wayland, 1987)
Clark, Philip, *American Civil War* (Cherrytree Books, 1988)
Ross, Stewart, *A Soldier in World War One* (Wayland, 1987)
Ross, Stewart (ed), *The Second World War* (Wayland, 1987)
King, Dr John, *The Gulf War* (Wayland, 1991)

Timeline

Periods covered in this book and some of the major developments in weapons and tactics.

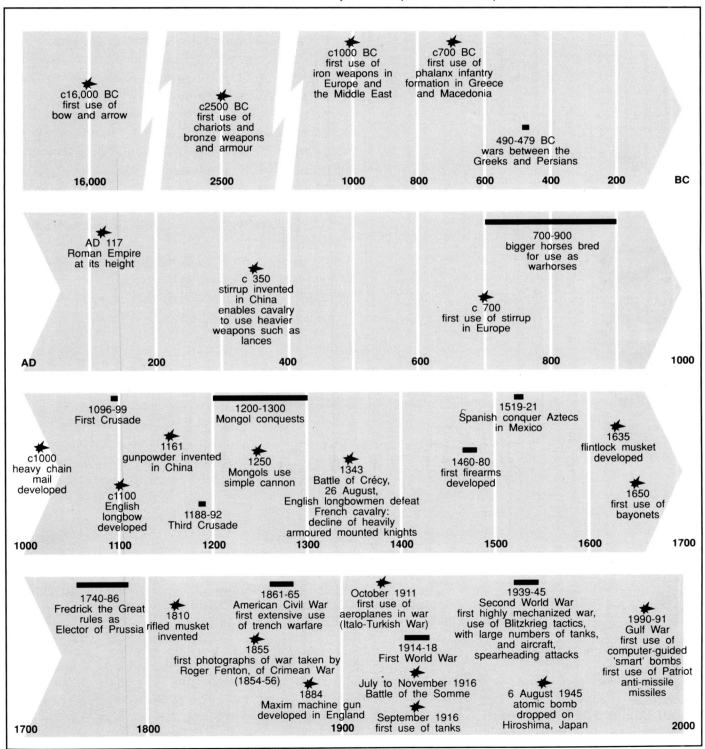

c16,000 BC
first use of
bow and arrow

c2500 BC
first use of
chariots and
bronze weapons
and armour

c1000 BC
first use of
iron weapons in
Europe and
the Middle East

c700 BC
first use of
phalanx infantry
formation in Greece
and Macedonia

490-479 BC
wars between the
Greeks and Persians

16,000   2500   1000   800   600   400   200   BC

AD 117
Roman Empire
at its height

c 350
stirrup invented
in China
enables cavalry
to use heavier
weapons such as
lances

700-900
bigger horses bred
for use as
warhorses

c 700
first use of stirrup
in Europe

AD   200   400   600   800   1000

1096-99
First Crusade

1200-1300
Mongol conquests

1519-21
Spanish conquer Aztecs
in Mexico

1635
flintlock musket
developed

c1000
heavy chain
mail
developed

1161
gunpowder invented
in China

1250
Mongols use
simple cannon

1343
Battle of Crécy,
26 August,
English longbowmen defeat
French cavalry:
decline of heavily
armoured mounted knights

1460-80
first firearms
developed

1650
first use of
bayonets

c1100
English
longbow
developed

1188-92
Third Crusade

1000   1100   1200   1300   1400   1500   1600   1700

1740-86
Fredrick the Great
rules as
Elector of Prussia

1810
rifled musket
invented

1861-65
American Civil War
first extensive use
of trench warfare

October 1911
first use of
aeroplanes in war
(Italo-Turkish War)

1939-45
Second World War
first highly mechanized war,
use of Blitzkrieg tactics,
with large numbers of tanks,
and aircraft,
spearheading attacks

1990-91
Gulf War
first use of
computer-guided
'smart' bombs
first use of Patriot
anti-missile
missiles

1855
first photographs of war taken by
Roger Fenton, of Crimean War
(1854-56)

1914-18
First World War

1884
Maxim machine gun
developed in England

July to November 1916
Battle of the Somme

September 1916
first use of tanks

6 August 1945
atomic bomb
dropped on
Hiroshima, Japan

1700   1800   1900   2000

Index

Sources of quotations

p.4. Thjodolf Arnorsson, fragment of a poem quoted by Snorri Sturluson in *Heimskringla* in the translation *King Harald's Saga* by Magnus Magnusson and Hermann Palsson, Penguin Books, 1966, pp.58–9. Pp.6, 7, 8 (top) Plutarch's quotations come from *Plutarch on Sparta*, a Penguin selection of Plutarch's writings including the Xenophon essay. P.8 (below). *Life of Agesilaus* is part of the *Age of Alexander* in a Penguin selection of *Plutarch's Lives*. P.10. Vegetius' quote is found in Yvon Garlan, *War in the Ancient World*, Chatto & Windus, 1975. P.16. Bernard of Clairvaux, *De laude novae militiae Sancti Bernardi Opera*, ed. J. Leclerq et al., Rome, 1963 III, p.214. The extract here is from L. and

J. Riley-Smith, *The Crusades: Idea and Reality 1094–1274*, E. Arnold, 1981, p.102. P.17. *Itinerarium regis Ricardi* is quoted by Elizabeth Hallam (ed) in *Chronicles of the Crusades*, Weidenfeld & Nicolson, 1989. P.18. The extract here is from the Penguin translation *The Travels of Marco Polo* by R.E. Latham, chapter two, pp.69–70. P.21. Ibn al-Athir (1160–1233) *Kamil at-Tawarikh* (The Perfect History or the Collection of Histories) is quoted by R. Grosset in *The Empire of the Steppes*, Rutgers University Press, 1970, p.262. P.26. Extract from Dr. Moore's *A View of Society and Manners in France, Switzerland and Germany*, 1789, Dublin. Vol II is taken from T. Lentin, *Frederick the Great*, Open

University Press, 1979. P.28. Letter to d'Alembert was in *Oeuvres de Frederick le Grand*, vol XXIV (1848), Berlin; quoted in T. Lentin, *Frederick the Great*, as above. Pp.30, 33. *The Life of Billy Yank* is by Bell Irvin Wiley, Charter Books, 1962. P.32. Quoted by Lloyd Lewis in *Sherman, Fighting Prophet*, Harcourt Brace and Co., New York 1932. P.35. Quoted by M. Middlebrook in *The First Day on the Somme*, Allen Lane 1971. P.37. Quoted by J. Simpkin in *Contemporary Accounts of the First World War*, Tressel, 1981. P.40 (top). *Hitler as Military Commander*, Sphere Books 1971. P.40 (below). Quoted by Alexander Werth in *Russia at War 1941–5*, Barrie and Rockliff, 1964.